## Other Titles From Dev Love Press

Love In Touch
The Boy Next Door
Harvard Hottie
Paradox
Devoted
(W)hole
Breath(e)

# You Can Write Characters with Physical Disabilities

DEV
LOVE
PRESS

You Can Write Characters with Physical Disabilities
1st Edition

Visit our website at **www.devlovepress.com**

ISBN: *978-0-9858263-4-5*

# Contents

# Why Include Characters with Disabilities?

As a writer, you know the importance of populating your world with a believable, diverse cast of characters. When all the people in your story look, walk, and talk like you, there's not much story going on. Your characters should have varied personalities, different weaknesses, and unique strengths. Sometimes, your character may need to have a disability. Here's a look at a few reasons to include disabled characters in your story.

## The Disability is Crucial to the Plot

Consider the 1999 film *At First Sight*. Val Kilmer plays Virgil Adamson, a character who has been blind since he was three years old. The movie, which is on one level a simple romance, draws plot points from the activity surrounding a radical surgery that returns Virgil's sight. The story explores Virgil's ups and downs as he struggles to live in a world he can suddenly see, then struggles with that fact that his sight might not last forever.

In *At First Sight*, the inclusion of the main character's disability is crucial to the plot. There *is no story* without the main character's blindness. Other stories that depend on a character with disabilities to drive certain essential elements of plot include *Rain Man*, Emlyn Chand's recent "Farsighted" YA series, Cynthia Voigt's award-winning *Izzy, Willy Nilly*, the classic *Flowers for Algernon*, and Alison Winfree Pickrell's *Unto the Least of These*.

Plot involves a character changing through the course of events. In each of the above stories, the character's change is irrevocably tied to his or her condition. Without the loss of her leg, Izzy would just be another cheerleader — without her disability, there's no struggle to fit in, no challenge to do normal things, no friendship with Rosamunde. In short, there's no book.

## The Disability Differentiates Your Character

Maybe your plot gets by without the disability, but you think it benefits your character. If you're writing a teen romance, then writing the leading young man in a wheelchair or writing the heroine with a shorter arm adds texture to the story and gives you a unique place to write from. It's important to make the disability organic to the story, though. You don't want the reader to be cognizant of the fact that you wrote a book and then transposed a disabled character onto the plot just to pull at the heartstrings.

## Bringing Attention to a Disability

In some cases, the author has a very personal struggle with a disability. The desire to share her struggle and success is what drove Helen Keller to write her autobiography, for example. Others may have loved ones with a disability and want to bring education, information, and awareness to light in the form of fiction. Although there's nothing wrong with having a message behind your story — almost all authors have something of the sort — make sure the disability fits within the story and that there is, in fact, a story being told.

## Just Because

The best reason of all is because some people have disabilities. It doesn't have to be the center of the plot. It doesn't have to even be part of the plot at all. Some people have disabilities and it doesn't have to be the central focus of his or her life.

When you create a story that has a diverse cast of characters, you make your book more realistic and believable.

A person in real life doesn't just have a disability in order to make a point. She just has it and then gets on with her life.

Telling a story that isn't focused on disability where some characters happen to have disabilities makes for a richer and more realistic book.


## Ensuring Your Story is Accurate

There's nothing that will set a scientist off faster than the misrepresentation of his field in literature. If you're a police officer reading a crime novel where the author hasn't done a lick of research, you may be offended or put off by the inaccurate portrayal of the police force. It's easy to alienate readers when you include inaccurate information or portrayals, even though your work is fiction.

When you include a disabled character in fiction, you could be helping to spread stereotypes and myths. Unless you're personally involved with a disability, you might not even realize that you're including inaccuracies; especially if you're basing your character on things you've read or seen on television.

For example, how many times has a blind character in a movie, television show, or story touched the face of someone else in order to become familiar or recognize them? You'd be hard pressed to find someone that hasn't seen this stereotype acted out in fictional form. If you know anyone who is blind, though, you realize this rarely happens. Blind persons don't walk around touching other peoples' faces, because that would be rude and inappropriate. Just because someone can't see doesn't mean they don't have good manners.

The resources in this book have been gathered to help you include accurate, realistic characters with disabilities in your stories and novels. You'll find a resource section on several common disabilities as well as essays on avoiding misconceptions and clichés.

# Notes on Specific Disabilities

## Blindness

Complete blindness is a total loss of vision, which can be caused by diabetes, macular degeneration, cataracts, glaucoma, or birth defects. People can be born blind, struck blind by certain ailments, or develop blindness over time, usually in old age. Although it's not completely unheard of for someone to develop visual impairment following a traumatic accident, this is actually less common than some people think. A violent accident is more likely to injure an individual in a number of other ways, barring the involvement of something that cuts or strikes the eyes.

Individuals with legal blindness may have some ability to see shapes, images, and colors. The diagnosis of legal blindness requires a visual acuity of 20/200. A person with normal vision can see an object at 200 feet, but a person with legal blindness can only see the object at 20 feet. In some cases, the legally blind person can't even see that far.

## Physical Effects

Obviously, the physical effect of blindness is impaired vision, but there are secondary effects that come with that loss, especially during the early period of living with blindness. You may not realize how important sight is to everything you do; the ability to see your surroundings provides hundreds of bits of information to your brain every second. Blind individuals don't have that information, which can be jarring to someone who was previously sighted. Even someone who has always been blind or been blind for years will react differently to spaces and situations, although they would have developed other ways of obtaining some necessary information.

Although technology has come a long way, someone who is blind doesn't have the same easy access to communication that sighted individuals enjoy. Special keyboards, braille, text-to-speech applications, and computers offer a chance for normal daily living, especially in the home, but those gadgets aren't available everywhere. Consider what a blind character would do when faced with a menu in a restaurant or an emergency situation in busy streets after dropping a cell phone.

Even verbal communication must change for blind persons. Experts estimate that 55 percent of regular communication is done through body language and visual cues. Without the ability to receive and process such cues, blind characters may be at a disadvantage in certain situations. Will the blind character understand that someone is angry or that the story just told was a joke? If that information is only conveyed through visual cues, possibly not.

Values will likely be impacted by a lack of site. Beauty is hard to appreciate when you can't see it, and for blind persons, the value of beauty could take on unexpected forms. Kindness may be valued above physical beauty. The sound or tone of a voice may be what gives the first impression. Compliments and interactions will follow naturally from this. A blind character is unlikely to say "You look nice this evening" in an unironic manner, but they may say "You smell nice today."

As much as we like to believe that we live in an equal society, there are things that a blind character isn't going to be able to do. All the tech in the current world isn't going to make a blind person a safe driver or a viable tennis partner. At the same time, there aren't as many limitations as you think on blind people in society today. Given the right technology, a blind person can work fulltime, live safely in a home alone, and go about all necessary daily acts of living without constant assistance.

## Adaptations and Equipment

From text-to-speech apps to the basic cane, equipment has been developed throughout the decades to help blind people live a fuller life. Here's a look at some of the common equipment a blind character might come into contact with.

### White Canes
Also known as guide canes, white canes fall into several categories. Each cane is used in a different manner and usually requires some level of training from a physical therapist or mobility expert. A white walking stick helps to support someone while walking, and the color is a signal that the person is visually impaired. These sticks are not used to guide the blind person and are not generally covered under insurance policies.

A symbol cane is held by the blind person to indicate disability and the need for assistance, while a long cane is used by the blind person to self-guide. The long cane is swept along the ground in an arc in front of the person, allowing the person to know when obstacles are in the path. A guide cane, on the other hand, is used closer to the body to notify the person about things like steps.

Of all the canes, the long cane requires the most training and takes the most practice to use properly.

## Reading Machines

OCR scanning technology means text-to-speech scanners can quickly scan hardcopy text and convert it to verbal speech. This allows blind individuals to read work documents or the Sunday newspaper, among other things. With audiobooks and online news readily available, it's unlikely someone would use a reading machine for something like fiction reading. However, if your character is involved in research that requires ancient books, for example, then he or she may need a reading machine.

## Computer Programs

There are a number of computer programs aimed at helping blind individuals lead normal lives. Something like Dragon Naturally Speaking, which converts the spoken word to onscreen text, would allow blind individuals to send and receive emails, write documents, or pen novels. Such programs may not be necessary, however, because many blind people can learn to touch type. Mousing would be a problem, since that requires hand-to-eye coordination. However, there are computer add-ons and operating systems that allow voice command operation for many functions.

**Mobile Apps**

A growing number of mobile apps also leverage technology to assist the visually impaired. Recently, a blind inventor from England launched an app that uses a mobile phone camera to convert text to electronic speech.

Other adaptations for the blind include the publication of major signs in braille, auditory kiosks in many public places like shopping malls and museums, tactile tablets, and even photovoltaic retinal prosthesis that can restore limited sight loss to patients who suffer from degenerative retinal conditions.

## Common Misunderstandings

Almost all blind individuals can tell the difference between light and dark. Even most of the 18 percent of visually impaired individuals who meet the requirements for complete blindness can still tell you if there's a spotlight shining on them or whether they're in a dark or light room.

Most blind individuals who learn braille as an adult aren't going to be breezing through lengthy books. It's a second language, after all, and most blind individuals who know braille are only fluent enough to read basic signs and labels. Most blind people don't rely on a guide dog; guide dogs are extremely expensive to train and are not usually covered under insurance programs.

Blind individuals can hold many types of jobs, including many you may not think of. According to a report from the State of Iowa, blind persons currently hold jobs as administrative assistants, CEOs, cashiers, members of the clergy, housekeepers, human resource reps, lawyers, managers, music professors, and even veterinary technicians!

Contrary to pop culture, blind individuals don't develop a mysterious sixth sense. They don't even develop better senses of touch, hearing, or smell. Instead, they learn to use the sense they do have in better ways, which can give the impression of stronger senses.

# Deafness

Deafness is the inability to hear for whatever reason. When referring to the physical state, deafness encompasses all degrees of hearing loss known as borderline, moderate, severe, and profound. Age-related diminished hearing ability is common, while deafness caused by a virus or disease in modern times is rare. You are considered to be hard-of-hearing if the impairment is mild, and "Hearing Impaired" is the politically correct term for a deaf person these days. Many feel that it's implying a handicap, however, rather than a state of being. Often they would simply prefer to be called deaf.

### Physical Effects

Deafness that is present at birth is known as congenital. Acquired deafness manifests later in life, and may or may not be genetic. Congenital deafness is not always inherited. It could be due to an infection or other condition to which a mother was exposed while pregnant, such as measles.

Hearing loss can also be classified by which sections of the auditory system are involved in the problem. If it's the nervous system, the disability is known as sensorineural hearing loss. This type of hearing loss decreases the ability to differentiate consonant sounds, and responds well to hearing aids.

Conductive hearing loss occurs when the parts of the ear that transmit sound – the outer and middle ear – are affected. In this case, vowel sounds and lower frequencies may be the first sounds or only sounds the individual loses access to. Medical treatment sometimes corrects the problem.

Some individuals experience mixed hearing loss, which is a combination of sensorineural and conductive issues.

Conditions that can lead to temporary, long-term, or permanent hearing loss include:

- Meniere's disease (affects inner ear fluids)
- Hearing loss due to aging
- Nerve injury from syphilis
- Hearing loss of unknown cause (idiopathic hearing loss)
- Nerve tumors
- Drug toxicity (such as aspirin and aminoglycosides).
- Ear wax blocking the ear canal
- Otitis media (middle ear infection or inflammation)
- Otosclerosis (new bone formation in the middle ear)

There are a wide range of symptoms related to deafness. Mild loss of high frequency hearing, tinnitus (commonly known as ringing in the ears), or complete deafness can develop over time. The physical effects can be directly related to both the actual lack of hearing and dealing with the symptoms of the condition causing the deafness.

Stress-related symptoms include headaches, high blood pressure, and muscle pain from tension or depression. People who are developing hearing loss may withdraw from family and friends because it becomes difficult to take part in conversations. They find it annoying to constantly ask others to repeat what they said. The need for television volume to be turned up to uncomfortable levels disrupts everyone's relaxation and is frustrating. Tiredness, eating and sleeping problems, and low self-esteem can lead to anxiety, self-criticism, and sexual problems. These are all issues you might explore with a deaf character, but remember that someone who has always been deaf or has been deaf for a long time is less likely to experience such emotions than someone who has recently lost some or all of his hearing.

Damage to the development of speech, language, and cognitive skills in children born deaf or who develop hearing loss during infancy has a lifelong effect creating immense difficulties. The earlier the detection of a child's hearing loss, the better the chance for maximum development.

## Adaptations and Equipment

When hearing loss is not medically treatable in a child, amplifying hearing aids and communication development strategies can be used beginning even in young infants. Technological advancements have opened doors that were previously inaccessible.

Children have a greater chance of successful treatment and quality of life improvement because they don't have the psychological impediments that older folks, and even adolescents, have.

Much of the challenge in adapting to hearing loss comes from a refusal to acknowledge the problem rather than limits of technology. Once a person with hearing loss gets past a self-perception problem, remarkable tools become available to improve hearing capability in so many ways—not only for enjoyment, but also to help with the ability to hold a job, care for a family, and be independent in day-to-day circumstances.

The number one adaptation people think of when it comes to deafness is a hearing aid. There are a substantial number of available styles, but all serve the same purpose: to carry sound into your ear. Some are small enough to fit in the ear canal, making them almost invisible. Others fit partially, while many designs are custom styled for an open fit behind the ear. Almost all of them are digital and are found in prices ranging from several hundred dollars to several thousand dollars. Some private insurance policies cover part or all of the cost; Medicare does not. Elderly individuals may be able to obtain hearing aids through Medicare supplement plans, but in many cases, they must purchase the devices themselves.

Adaptive equipment allows people with disabilities to handle much of their daily living on their own. Other technologies to improve the quality of life for the deaf includes:

- Telephone adapters
- Bluetooth technology within hearing aids to be used with cell phones and other Bluetooth-capable devices
- Electronic cochlear implant devices to partially restore hearing lost due to inner ear damage
- Assistive Listening Systems for students where an instructor wears a microphone that broadcasts to the student's receiver, or via FM
- C-Print, a speech-to-text system

Vibrating alarm clocks and signalers like pendants or watches for doorbells, baby monitors, telephones, and oven timers Software for the Deaf, computer programs designed to improve the lives of people with hearing disabilities with mechanisms such as animated deaf signers, educational visual presentations that interpret audio messages and data, and simple teaching tools for children

Technology can be very expensive. Basic adaptive equipment is often paid for by private health insurance or Medicaid, at least in part. State agencies provide money to meet children's needs, and senior support services in many states provide financial assistance. Private organizations such as the Alexander Graham Bell Foundation Association offer grants to qualifying disabled individuals when criteria are met.

## Common Misunderstandings and Misconceptions

Hearing people often have preconceived ideas about what deaf people are like. Much of what is believed is based on television and books. For example, not all deaf people use American Sign Language (in fact there are also different Sign Languages in different countries). Just like any other skill, sign language the personal choice of an adult or a child's parents. When writing deaf characters, you as the author must make this choice and understand what it means for the story.

You also need to know that sign language isn't just a conversion of English into word-for-word hand motions. Sign language has its own grammar, culture, history, terminology and characteristics. It is a secondary language.

Hearing aids don't solve every hearing-impaired problem. First, all hearing aids are not created equal. They are designed to assist with particular needs like eliminating background noise or dealing with low frequencies. Speaking too loudly can cause distortion for example, so your words may be heard, but not clearly enough to be understood. This type of issue could lead to misunderstandings or problems for your character.

You don't need an interpreter present in your story for every interaction between a deaf and hearing person. Depending on your characters other attributes, he or she may be able to communicate via body language, writing, hand signals and a variety of other methods. Just don't assume very deaf person reads lips. It's a very difficult skill and even the best at it have a low percentage of accuracy.

Remember that deaf people aren't necessarily mute people. Speech ability and quality are directly related to when the deafness occurred. Also, many deaf people are able to talk but choose not to because regulating volume, pitch, or sound of the voice is difficult.

Most importantly, remember that there is no relationship between hearing loss and intelligence. Deaf people can be successful in many professions, and many do not even consider themselves to be disabled. Instead, they share a unique culture. They drive cars, have families, and lead loving, productive lives.

## Note on Deaf With a Capital "D"

When someone calls him or herself Deaf it indicates belonging to the Deaf culture, which is seen by those individuals as a linguistic minority and not a disability. People who identify in this way do not view being able to hear as an advantage and often feel that the world needs to adapt to accept them rather than expecting them to want to be hearing.

# Spinal Muscular Atrophy

Spinal muscular atrophy is a group of genetic diseases that cause muscle wasting in the limbs of babies and children. The disease is caused by problems with the SMN1 gene, which produces a protein that helps motor neurons function properly. Some people with spinal muscular atrophy are missing the gene, while others have a defective copy of the gene. Without the necessary protein, the lower motor neurons break down and die.

There are three different types of this disease. SMA is classified according to the severity of the symptoms and how old a person is at the time of onset. Type I affects babies at birth or within a few months of birth. This type of SMA is also called Werdnig-Hoffman disease. Type II affects children ranging from 6 to 18 months of age. Type III, referred to as Kugelberg-Welander disease, usually affects the lower extremities. The symptoms typically appear between the ages of 2 and 17.

## Physical Effects

Spinal muscular atrophy causes a breakdown of the connections between the nerve cells and the muscles. The physical effects of the disease depend on the person's age. A baby with type I will likely have weak muscles, reduced muscle tone, and problems breathing or feeding. Think about how a character might have to adapt to these challenges during a baby's first few months of life. A baby that has feeding problems may need supplemental nutrition to ensure proper growth.

Babies and young children with spinal muscular atrophy may be unable to control their movements, especially head movements. Weakness usually starts in the leg muscles or shoulders, but it tends to get worse as the disease progresses. Young children with this disease may have difficulty maintaining normal posture. Frequent respiratory infections are another potential complication of spinal muscular atrophy. Children with SMA may have difficulty with or be unable to participate in normal activities like attending school, developing basic motor skills, or progressing with language skills.

One thing people fail to consider is the effects of adult SMA on a person's sex life. An adult with SMA may not be able to perform acrobatic bedroom moves, but there are ways partners can work together to make the experience a good one. Reclining chairs might make it easier to maintain some positions. An enthusiastic partner can also help the person with SMA focus on intimacy and pleasure rather than the limitations of the disease.

In some cases, spinal muscular atrophy does lead to the premature death of an infant or child. This is most common in cases of type I SMA, but it can occur in other types. If you include a character with infant or childhood SMA, then you'll need to accommodate for how the disability impacts family life. Parents must live daily with the knowledge that their child is unlikely to grow into adulthood; what type of changes does that make in the character's dynamic? The parent may be more likely to splurge on today's luxury for the child than to save for college, for example. SMA and the associated stresses are also likely to alter relationships between couples, between parents and other children, and between the family and the outside world.

## Adaptations and Equipment

The effects of spinal atrophy vary over time, so there are a number of adaptive devices and pieces of equipment available to help those with the disease. Some of these devices improve mobility, while others make it easier to manage respiratory problems and feeding issues.

### Wheelchairs
Many people with spinal muscular atrophy may use wheelchairs to get around. (For children, these chairs also make it easier for parents, grandparents, and other family members to transport their kids to school and other places outside the home). Some people with SMA have two wheelchairs; they pick which one they will use depending on the circumstances. A heavy motorized chair might be perfect for everyday use, but a lightweight chair is a better option for traveling. Travel chairs can usually be disassembled so they do not take up much space in a vehicle.

### Walkers and Braces

Some people with SMA are able to walk, but they may need walkers or braces for support. These assistive devices make it easier to stay balanced and maintain a good posture when walking.

### Household Adaptations

Houses can be renovated to accommodate the needs of a person with SMA. Wider doors and ramps make it easier to get in and out of the house with a wheelchair. When designing bathrooms for people with SMA and similar diseases, it is best to make the shower level with the ground. A shower chair and adjustable showerhead make it easier for a person with SMA to perform personal hygiene activities. Putting cabinets, door handles, and shelves lower than usual limits the difficulties someone using a wheelchair will have when trying to prepare meals or perform household cleaning activities.

### Common Misconceptions

A common misconception regarding spinal muscular atrophy is that people with the disease have no sensation or limited sensation. It really depends on the person. Some people do have some sensation problems, but others have the same ability to sense stimuli as people who do not have spinal muscular atrophy. SMA is not paralysis.

Some people also make the mistake of assuming people with SMA also have cognitive disabilities. Someone with SMA could have additional disabilities such as learning disabilities, but they are a separate issue. Many people with SMA are of normal intelligence and are able to learn new information easily. With the right adaptations, it is possible for someone with SMA to attend college classes or learn vocational skills they can use to obtain employment.

Many individuals will speak to a parent or caregiver instead of directing communication to someone who has SMA. This may be a problem that comes up for your character, but as the author, you should know whether or not your character is able to handle his own communication. Many individuals with SMA are.

Because spinal muscular atrophy is a progressive disease, it does limit life expectancy. You would not want to create an 85-year-old character with spinal muscular atrophy, as this wouldn't be very realistic. People with spinal muscular atrophy may also have to use special equipment to breathe and get the nutrition they need (such as a gastrostomy tube). It is important to describe the equipment accurately and explain the purpose of each machine. A common misconception is that people with the disease have to use special equipment at all times. This may be the case for some people, but other people may only have to use their equipment at certain times of the day.

Assuming that someone with SMA cannot have a fulfilling sex life is also a common mistake. People with SMA want to be loved and have relationships with other people, just like people without SMA. With the right adaptations and a caring partner, it is possible for someone with this disease to lead a fulfilling sex life. The person might need to use pillows, wedges, or other items to prop up body parts and make things more comfortable. An understanding partner may have to help with transfer into and out of a wheelchair, but this should not diminish the quality of the encounter. People with SMA need to be educated about sexual health just like people who do not have the disease.

# Multiple Sclerosis

Multiple sclerosis is an immune system disease that attacks the spinal cord, brain, and optic nerves. What makes this disease so different from other medical conditions is that it is very unpredictable. Some people experience mild symptoms, while others experience paralysis or blindness. When the immune system attacks the components of the central nervous system, the protective covering of the nerve fibers becomes damaged. This disrupts the nerve impulses that usually travel between the spinal cord and brain.

Progressive-relapsing multiple sclerosis affects only 5 percent of people with the disease. People with this form of MS get worse right from the beginning and experience attacks on their neurological function as the disease progresses.

Approximately 85 percent of those with MS are initially diagnosed with a form of the disease called relapsing-remitting multiple sclerosis. This form of the disease causes "clearly defined" attacks on a person's neurological function. Each attack is followed by a remission, or complete recovery period.

Primary-progressive MS causes slowly worsening neurologic function, with some people experiencing minor improvements or plateaus. People with this form of the disease do not experience distinct remissions. Secondary-progressive MS usually develops after an initial diagnosis of relapsing-remitting MS. This causes the disease to worsen steadily.

## Physical Effects

The physical effects of multiple sclerosis are very different from one person to another, so it is important to keep this in mind when developing characters with the disease. One of the most common effects is abnormal sensations such as burning, itching, stabbing, numbness, and tearing pains. Approximately 50 percent of the people with multiple sclerosis have these symptoms, and they are physical effects that would be easy to explore in a character's thoughts and actions.

Some people with multiple sclerosis develop bowel and bladder problems. This is because normal bladder and bowel function depend on the brain's ability to communicate with the spinal cord. When multiple sclerosis affects the transmission of nerve impulses, incontinence and other elimination problems might develop. Some of the symptoms of bladder dysfunction in people with MS include frequent urination, increased nighttime urination, urinary urgency, and incontinence. People with MS might also experience bouts of diarrhea, bowel incontinence, or constipation due to the disruption of normal electrical impulses. Think about how bowel and bladder problems might affect a character's self-confidence or ability to participate in a romantic relationship.

Fatigue, dizziness, muscle spasms, and trouble walking are some of the other physical effects someone with multiple sclerosis might experience. About 80 percent of people with the disease experience fatigue at some point. The fatigue usually worsens in the afternoon and evening, and it doesn't seem to be related to the amount of work a person performs during the day. Fatigue can be associated with sleepiness, muscle weakness, and difficulty thinking.

Dizziness is common, but it should not be confused with vertigo. Most people with MS do not feel like the room is spinning around them. Muscle spasms affect about 40 percent of the people with early MS symptoms and 60 percent of those who have been diagnosed with progressive MS. The spasms may be mild, or they may be strong and painful. Muscle spasms, weakness, numbness, and fatigue may combine to make walking difficult for some people with MS. Keep these physical effects in mind when writing scenes involving work or leisure activities.

## Adaptations and Equipment

The goal of using adaptive equipment is to make people with MS more independent and help them enjoy their lives as much as possible. These are just some of the adaptations and equipment available to people with multiple sclerosis.

### Kitchen Tools

When the brain and spinal cord cannot communicate with each other, it can be difficult to grasp objects or perform repetitive movements. Several kitchen tools make it easier for someone with MS to prepare meals. Someone with MS will likely have an easier time using an electric can opener than a manual one. Rocker knives are available to reduce the number of wrist motions needed to slice foods. These knives are also helpful for people who have reduced arm strength. A tool called a reacher makes it easier to pick up objects that are on high shelves or sitting on top of the refrigerator.

### Cleaning Tools

Cleaning a home is more of a workout than you might realize. Wheeled carts are ideal for storing cleaning supplies as they can be moved without a lot of effort.

Long-handled brooms and dusters eliminate the need to climb on a stepstool to dust a tall bookshelf or clean the blades of a ceiling fan.

## Mobility Devices

For those affected by muscle weakness, pain, and fatigue, mobility devices make it easier to participate in social activities or do basic tasks like grocery shopping and going to the dentist. Braces, walkers, and canes are available for those who need help balancing themselves as they walk. Orthotics, or shoe inserts, help improve stability and may even help relieve fatigue in some people with multiple sclerosis. Those with progressive MS can use electric wheelchairs or scooters to get around. Power chairs are an option that may be covered by insurance if the individual is no longer ambulatory and does not have the upper body ability to use a manual chair. Caregivers might use lifts and transfer boards to help people with MS get into and out of vehicles, beds, or bathtubs.

## Clothing Adaptations

Closing buttons and zippers might be difficult for someone who has weakness in the hands. Clothing can be adapted with Velcro and other materials to eliminate the need to struggle with buttons when getting dressed. Bending over to tie shoelaces may also be difficult, especially during an MS flare, so slip-on shoes are a good alternative.

## Reading and Writing Tools

Muscle weakness and stiffness make it difficult for some people to hold books or writing implements. Book holders make it possible to read comfortably, while pencil grips and other writing aids make it easier to write. Many educational organizations are incorporating tablet technology and computers, providing additional ways for disability people, such as those with MS, to engage with learning material and communicate with teachers or other students.

**Common Misconceptions**
Some people think multiple sclerosis reduces life expectancy. Experts from the Multiple Sclerosis Foundation say the life expectancy for people with MS is no different from the life expectancy of those unaffected by MS. Because there are older people living with the disease, you do not have to make a character with MS 20 or 30 years old, although you will need to consider how the disease impacts long-term life quality and daily activity for characters of any specific age. There are some variants of the disease that may shorten someone's lifespan, but they are quite rare.

One of the most common misconceptions about this disease is that it can be diagnosed right away. In its early stages, multiple sclerosis might cause numbness or tingling. In some cases, MRI scans and other tests cannot find any lesions to explain these symptoms. Some patients do not receive their diagnoses for years after they report their initial symptoms. This is because the disease is progressive and difficult to diagnose.

Another common misconception about multiple sclerosis is that it cannot be treated. This is simply not true. Although there is no known cure for the disease, there are several medications that can slow the progression of MS and improve the quality of life of those affected by the disease. Some medications also help control bowel and bladder problems, fatigue, or muscle stiffness caused by multiple sclerosis. Multiple sclerosis can also be managed with lifestyle changes, a healthful diet, and regular physical activity. You should not assume that someone with multiple sclerosis will end up using a wheelchair. Some do, but there are others who live their entire lives without even having to use assistive devices to walk.

# Cerebral Palsy

Cerebral palsy is a group of disorders that affect body movement. Although the condition cannot be cured, it usually doesn't get worse as a person ages. Cerebral palsy develops as the result of brain damage sustained during fetal development or within a short time after birth. People with cerebral palsy may also have difficulty maintaining their balance or normal posture. The effects of cerebral palsy vary based on the extent of the brain damage and the treatments used to help children improve their motor skills.

Genetic abnormalities, maternal infections, congenital brain malformations, and fetal injury are all potential causes of cerebral palsy. In some cases, medical professionals are unable to determine the exact cause of the disorder. Periventricular leukomalacia, or damage to the brain's white matter, interferes with the transmission of signals in the nervous system. Cerebral dysgenesis is the medical term for abnormal brain development. This also interferes with the transmission of brain signals. If a developing baby does not get enough oxygen to the brain, this can also cause cerebral palsy.

## Physical Effects

The physical effects of cerebral palsy vary based on the extent of the brain damage and the age of the person affected. In babies younger than 6 months old, stiffness might be one of the most obvious physical effects. A baby with cerebral palsy may also feel floppy when you pick him up. In babies 6 to 10 months of age, cerebral palsy makes it difficult to roll over, touch the hands to the mouth, and touch one hand to the other. Consider what a character might do if she noticed her child had difficulty crawling or reaching other milestones.

As a baby with cerebral palsy becomes a toddler, other signs of the disorder may begin to show up. They include a lack of muscle coordination, weakness in one or more of the limbs, muscle stiffness, exaggerated reflexes, muscle tightness, scissored gait, walking on the toes, shaking, excessive drooling, difficulty writing or handling small objects, and difficulty speaking or swallowing. A parent noticing these signs for the first time would have a very different reaction from the parent excited about his child's progress with crawling or walking.

Cerebral palsy also affects the way adults function. The disorder puts extra stress on the body, so some adults might experience premature aging of the lungs, blood vessels, and heart. Some adults experience joint compression and limited movement as the result of cerebral palsy. This can lead to degenerative arthritis, nerve entrapment, and other degenerative conditions. Pain in the knees, hips, upper back, ankles, and lower back may also be present. Something people take for granted, such as using an e-reader, may be difficult for an adult who has trouble moving her hands or arms. Think about how a character would have to adapt to workplace tasks such as typing, using a photocopier, or operating a multi-line telephone system.

The effects of cerebral palsy vary considerably. While some people may only have slight tremors, others need power wheelchairs and may have difficulty speaking or be unable to speak. One frequently seen effect of cerebral palsy is hands that are bent down sharply at the wrists.

## Adaptations and Equipment

Assistive devices help people with cerebral palsy reduce activity limitations and improve their quality of life. These devices make it possible to participate in work or leisure activities, increasing independence and helping people build self-esteem. Here is an overview of some of the devices a character with cerebral palsy might use to overcome physical challenges.

### Writing Aids

Tremors make it difficult to hold a pen or pencil and write steadily. There are several tools available to help people with cerebral palsy communicate in writing. They include Ergowriter, Steady Write, and RinG-Pen. Ergowriter makes it easier to position the thumb when holding a standard pen or pencil. Steady Write has a triangular base that helps balance the hand. This tool can help people with shaky handwriting write more legibly. The RinG-Pen tool makes it easier to grip a writing instrument properly.

### Wheelchairs

There are several different types of wheelchairs available to increase mobility. A basic wheelchair usually has a leg rest and arms. The seats come in widths of 16 to 20 inches on most models. Lightweight chairs are a good option for traveling.

The lightweight construction makes it easier to get the chair into and out of a vehicle, and this type of chair may also include an adjustable-height back or quick-release wheels. Motorized wheelchairs are ideal for those who have difficulty using their arms. There are a number of accessories people can buy for their wheelchairs, from extra wheels to seat pads.

**Adapted Vehicles and Car Seats**
Parents in the United States have to follow special regulations when traveling with children who have physical disabilities. In some cases, an adaptive car seat is required. These seats keep the children upright and increase their comfort, making them safer as they travel. An adapted vehicle makes it easier to travel with a child who uses a wheelchair. An adapted vehicle may also make it possible for an adult with cerebral palsy to drive. Some adapted vehicles, for example, have hand controls.

**Mechanical Lifts**
Weakness in the legs may make it difficult for someone with cerebral palsy to use stairs. Mechanical chairs and lifts make it easier to adapt to homes, schools, and workplaces with multiple levels and no elevators. A mechanical lift makes it easier to get into bed or use the bathtub, while a chair lift allows someone with leg weakness to go up and down the stairs safely. These devices also increase independence and reduce reliance on other people. In many cases, so-called "optional" devices are not covered by insurance, but may be partially covered through assistance programs.

**Computer Applications**

Technology has made it much easier for people with disabilities to adapt. Many mobile applications are available to help people with cerebral palsy communicate. There are also educational apps available to help children improve their speech and fine motor skills.

**Common Misconceptions**
One of the most common misconceptions about cerebral palsy is that it is genetic. This is not a disorder that can be passed from one generation to another. A mother would not be able to have a genetic test to find out if her baby would be born with cerebral palsy. This is because the brain damage that causes cerebral palsy does not occur until sometime during development or shortly after birth.

Some people automatically assume that everyone with cerebral palsy has a learning disability. This could not be farther from the truth. Though it is caused by brain damage, it does not affect intelligence. Some people with cerebral palsy do have learning disabilities, but these are separate from the physical disability of cerebral palsy. People with this disorder can attend regular schools, go to college, and build rewarding careers. Dr. Janice Brunstrom has cerebral palsy, but she was able to become one of the leading scientists studying the disorder. Abbey Curran has cerebral palsy and competed in the Miss USA Pageant in 2008.

People also make the mistake of assuming that cerebral palsy is the same for everyone. Some people experience very mild effects of cerebral palsy. They may have some weakness in one of the arms or have difficulty holding a pen without shaking. Other people have more serious problems, usually because they sustained more extensive brain damage. These people might have difficulty walking or talking.

# Muscular Dystrophy

Muscular dystrophy is actually a group of diseases, not a single condition. As a genetic condition, it is linked to genes and heredity, but some of the gene mutations that cause muscular dystrophy can occur in the developing embryo or even the mother's egg. This means genetic testing is not always going to reveal risks associated with the condition.

The most common version of this condition is usually found in younger boys, though the disease can impact people of any race, sex, or age. A family history of the condition increases a person's risk.

Since there are more than thirty forms of muscular dystrophy, it's important to define what type of condition a character has. This is going to inform your decision as a writer about symptoms, characteristics, and needs for your character.

The most common form of MD is Duchenne, which makes up about 50 percent of MD cases. The condition involves a protein deficiency that weakens muscles and increases the risk of muscle injury. This form of MD is usually diagnosed in boys from ages 3 to 5.

For adults, the most common form of MD is Myotonic. This condition has a type 1 and type 2 form and involves an unusually large repetition of certain components in the genetic structure of a person's DNA. Myotonic MD is generally diagnosed in adults aged 20 through 30.

Here's a quick chart of some of the more common forms of MD, but remember to do additional research for any character as symptomology and other details will be different for each. Many of these forms of MD can strike persons outside of the high-risk group.

| Type of Muscular Dystrophy | Generally Diagnosed In |
|---|---|
| Duchenne | Boys age 3 to 5 |
| Becker | Males age 11 to 25 |
| Myotonic | Adults age 20 to 30 |
| Congenital | Infants up to age 2 |
| Emery-Dreifuss | People age 10 to mid-20s |
| Facioscapulohumeral | Teens of both genders, but has been diagnosed in individuals as old as 40 |
| Limb-girdle | Adolescents and young adults |
| Distal | People age 40 to 60 |
| Oculopharyngeal | People age 40 to 50 |

**Physical Effects**

The physical effects of MD depend on the type of condition present and how bad the genetic mutation is. Here's a look at common physical effects for each of the forms of MD listed above.

**Duchenne**
- Weakness in legs and pelvis
- Increased risk of falls
- Trouble getting up from a sitting or lying position
- Difficulty with basic physical activity like running
- A noticeable waddle in gait
- Fat accumulation that makes calf muscles look large

## Becker

- Individual may walk on toes
- Increased risk of falls
- Difficulty getting up from floor
- Muscle cramps

## Myotonic

- Difficulty swallowing
- Vision problems, including cataracts or drooping lids
- Weight loss
- Balding at the front of the head
- Drowsiness
- Excessive sweating
- Heart problems
- Infertility
- Impotence
- Irregular menstrual periods

## Congenital

- Difficulty swallowing
- Difficulty breathing
- Foot deformities
- Intellectual disabilities
- Scoliosis
- Poor joint movement due to shortening of muscles
- Poor motor function
- Poor motor control

## Emery-Dreifuss

- Poor joint movement due to shortening of muscles
- Elbows may lock in a flexed position
- Shoulder deterioration
- Individual may walk on toes
- Rigidity in spine
- Weakness in facial muscles, which is usually mild

## Facioscapulohumeral
- Slanted or winged shoulders due to muscle wasting
- Poor bicep and tricep reflex
- Difficulty swallowing
- Difficulty chewing
- Difficulty speaking
- Hearing impairment
- Curved spine

## Limb-girdle
- Increased risk of falls
- Weakness in hips, shoulders, neck, and legs
- Trouble standing from chairs or walking on steps
- Trouble carrying items
- Noticeable waddle in gait
- Rigidity in spine

## Distal
- Reduce or no ability to use hands
- Inability to extend fingers
- Trouble with steps
- Trouble walking

## Oculopharyngeal
- Trouble swallowing
- Vision problems, including dropping lids
- Muscle weakness or wasting in shoulders, neck, and limbs
- Heart issues

Depending on the form of MD, individuals may be wheelchair bound by an early age. Struggling with basic movements — whether or not your character is in a wheelchair — is going to inform his entire outlook on the world. Where a healthy character may simply leave one room or building and travel to another, a character with MD would have to consider the need for assistance, mobility equipment, or alternative routes. He may be challenged by a plot point as simple as a broken elevator; it's always important to challenge any character, but make sure you don't solve all his problems by introducing another, healthy character to save the day. Most individuals with MD are capable of high levels of problem solving and can often discover inventive ways to deal with problems.

## Equipment and Adaptations

Just as MD conditions feature a wide range of diagnosis and physical symptoms, there are a range of medical devices meant to reduce symptoms and help those with MD live more normal lives. Some of the most common items are listed below.

### Standing from a Chair

From lifting armchairs to cushioned assisting devices, there are dozens of products that help individuals lift from a sitting to standing position. Lifting armchairs are usually powered by an electric motor and tilt forward until the person's feet touch the ground. The motor portion of these chairs may be reimbursable through insurance, including Medicare, although the cost of the armchair itself is usually paid for by the patient.

Individuals in the workforce or students can get special task chairs with lifting seats to help them stand. There are also chairs with battery-operated rising and lowering mechanisms. These allow individuals to lower the seat to a comfortable height for rising and sitting, but they can then raise the seat to a viable height for typing or working at a desk or table. Some chairs are designed so that, when the seat is lowered, individuals can "walk" the chair with their feet, moving around an office to access various work stations, printers, or other essential items without rising so many times during the day.

**Sitting from a Lying Position**
There are inflatable devices used by assistants or family members to help someone who has fallen. The fallen person is maneuvered over the device, which is then inflated. This pushes the person into a sitting position, making it easier to rise.

**Bathroom Fixtures**
Frames can be purchased that go over an existing toilet. The frames rise to assist individuals in sitting and standing. Some frames don't rise at all, but offer a more suitable position. Toilet seats that lift at an angle are usually not suitable for use by individuals with MD.

Shower chairs and seats offer safety, allowing those with MD to sit while taking a shower. Standard shower chairs may pose a problem for individuals with MD, as it can be difficult to rise from them. Wall-mounted shower chairs with a motorized lifting mechanism are more suitable. There are also companies that design specialty baths with built-in electrical or manual-motion seats.

Shower and wall rails may also be an important safety component for someone with MD, and allow someone in a wheelchair to maneuver in the restroom if they still have optimal functioning in upper limbs.

## Wheelchairs

Since some forms of MD impact children at a young age and can result in a loss of ambulation early in life, wheelchairs are an essential adaptation for many individuals. From manual chairs that are pushed by parents to electric chairs that can be operated by the individual, there are literally thousands of combinations of parts and functions.

It's important for families or individuals dealing with MD to consider both current and future needs. Children with MD are still growing, and are likely to outgrow early childhood chairs. You can't, however, put your character into a chair he'll "grow into," as an improperly sized chair can lead to injury and developmental issues.

Power chairs are driven by electronics, removing the need for someone to push the chair or for the individual to move the chair by rolling the wheels. Power chairs are a common adaptation for individuals with MD because they often lack appropriate muscle strength and control to maneuver a manual chair. Power chairs are *not* the same thing as mobility scooters; they are more technical pieces of equipment that must be fit by an experienced physical therapist and prescribed by a medical doctor. In cases with a doctor and therapist have certified the essential need of a power chair, many insurance companies will pay for all or a portion of the equipment cost. In the case of patients with MD, power chairs may come with options like powered seat, arm, and leg-rest adjustment.

Most insurances require a letter of medical necessity stating that an individuals is both unable to walk and unable to operate a manual chair before they will consider paying for a power chair. There are programs and organizations that offer financial support, assisting individuals with MD in covering out-of-pocket expenses related to power chairs and other equipment.

Other equipment and adaptations for individuals with MD include braces, assistive walking devices, and learning software or programs for children. Ramps to allow wheelchair-access to home, school, and office are important, as well as extra-wide doors.

## Common Misconceptions

One of the biggest misconceptions about MD is that it's a single condition, which you've already seen isn't true. Another misconception is that individuals with MD are less intelligent or mentally challenged. Although this may be the case in some instances, most individuals with MD who reach teen or adult years are of average intelligence; just as with a healthy group, you'll also have some who are below average or above average intellect.

Another myth is that people die of MD because they never get better. Although there are life-expectancy reducing forms of MD — especially those that come with higher cardiac risks — many individuals live long, normal, and otherwise healthy lives. Modern innovations in equipment, medicine, and surgery can even reduce or stave off some symptoms associated with the condition.

Not all individuals with MD are shut-ins or live "on the edge" of society. Individuals with MD — even those that are wheelchair bound — regularly participate in normal activities like working, socializing, going to school, dining out, attending concerts, and even camping. Although it may take a bit of extra planning, there's no reason individuals with MD can't get involved in any number of activities.

In most cases, sexual function is not diminished for someone with MD, although physical function is limited. Equipment that helps with movement and an understanding — but enthusiastic — partner can overcome such barriers.

# Spina Bifida

Spina bifida is a birth defect that affects the neural tube, which is what eventually develops into the brain and spinal cord as well as the surrounding tissues. The neural tube is usually formed and closed within the first month of a pregnancy, but for someone with spina bifida, the tube does not develop or close correctly.

There are four types of spina bifida; some facts about each are summarized below.

### Occulta
- Mildest and most common
- One or more vertebrae are deformed by a layer of skin that covers the vertebrae
- 10 to 20 percent of the population has this form
- Rarely causes symptoms

### Closed neural tube defects
- Group of different defects which create various deformities in the spine
- Few or no symptoms in most cases
- Worst cases involve some paralysis and problems with bladder and/or bowel

### Meningocele
- An abnormal vertebrae opening causes spinal fluid or tissue to protrude
- Some people have no symptoms, others experience complete paralysis

## Myelomeningocele

- Most severe
- Spinal elements are exposed through an opening in spine
- Symptoms include partial or complete paralysis below the abnormality
- Can be severe enough to keep a person from walking
- May involve bladder and bowel problems

### Physical Effects

As you can probably tell from the information above, the symptoms of spina bifida vary widely from person to person. Most closed neural tube defects are discovered by physicians when the individual is young, because they are generally accompanied by a telltale tuft of hair or indentation at the site of the malformation. More severe forms of spina bifida may involve a fluid-filled protrusion (sac) on the back.

Daily life with spina bifida also varies greatly depending on the severity of the condition. Some individuals may experience very minor physical issues with little to no impairment when it comes to daily activities. On the opposite end of the spectrum are individuals who use wheelchairs or who have a severe loss in mental functioning. These cases are rarer, and most individuals with spina bifida have normal intelligence levels.

In some cases, a related condition known as Chiari II can cause difficulty with feeding, breathing and swallowing. This usually develops in children with the myelomeningocele form of spina bifida. It's important to be vigilant with children who have this condition, as choking can be a big hazard.

Newborns with myelomeningocele are at a higher risk of developing meningitis, which can cause brain injury and death. Children with myelomeningocele may have problems learning, and the constant exposure to medical treatments can cause allergies to latex to develop over the years, which is important to remember if your character is using a condom during sexual activity. People with spina bifida may also develop skin issues, depression, or gastrointestinal issues.

Spina bifida can't be treated, because there is currently no way to restore damaged nerve and spinal tissue. Individuals with milder forms of the condition don't usually require any treatment and may live active, unencumbered lives. It's important for spina bifida to be diagnosed as early as possible — even while the fetus is still in the womb — so that medical staff can take action to prevent complications and infections. These complications often cause life-long issues for someone with spina bifida.

Between twenty and fifty percent of children with the more severe myelomeningocele form of spina bifida develop what is known as spinal cord tethering. This means the spinal cord attaches to bone or tissue that is not as mobile, stretching the spinal cord during the child's growth. The result of this issue can be paralysis of the legs and dysfunctional bladder and bowel. If the tethered spinal cord is found early, a surgery can correct the problem.

Depending on the type and severity of a person's condition, they may require numerous surgeries to correct symptoms associated with spina bifida. Surgeries on the hips, spine, and feet are common, and respiratory or swallowing problems are often treated with the installation of a shunt. Because catching and treating issues early greatly enhances the chance at long-term success, individuals with spina bifida may have experienced a number of procedures at a young age. Such a history is likely to impact your character in some way, whether it's created a dislike of hospital settings, an abnormal tolerance for pain, or a drive to become part of the medical field.

Even individuals with the occulta form of spina bifida can experience serious problems, especially if the location of their spinal malformation is in certain spots. Individuals with formation issues in some locations have been known to develop chronic kidney disease, for example.

Because of having paralysis and spinal cord issues from a young age, some individuals with spina bifida (particularly those who have been using a wheelchair from a young age) appear shorter and more compact than average. They may have a shorter torso or legs or appear to be unusually short in stature as an adult.

### Equipment and Adaptations

From shoes to seats, there are a number of items that can help someone with spina bifida enjoy an active, normal life. Remember that many people with this condition will not require any adaptations, as their symptoms are not present or limited. For others, here is a list of common equipment.

## Braces

For individuals—especially children—who have lost some muscle function in lower limbs, braces can help with walking and standing. In some cases, braces may be used to correct posture issues over time. In other cases, individuals may always walk with a brace, cane, or crutches to assist with support and balance.

## Adaptive Shoes

Customized shoes and inserts can help stabilize individuals with spina bifida. Perhaps more commonly, custom shoes create a more comfortable fit and walking experience when put on over braces or AFOs. It isn't all about comfort, though. Shoes that put pressure on braces could actually reduce the effect of the brace; constant pressure points will also create sores and blisters that could lead to long-term food problems or infection.

## Wheelchairs

When spina bifida results in paralysis of the lower limbs, individuals must rely on a wheelchair for mobility. Infant and toddler wheelchairs feature special designs for safety and to allow parents optimal functionality. These chairs are usually lightweight and may fold for easy portability. Some companies offer renovation services for homes and vehicles. They install ramps, widen doorways, and ensure flooring is appropriate for wheelchair use. Families can purchase ready-made vans with lifts and spaces to secure wheelchairs or can have their own vehicles modified to make it more convenient to load or unload vehicles.

Most individuals with spina bifida that become wheelchair bound have use of their upper body and limbs. This means they can maneuver a manual wheelchair, although they might need special seat cushions and backs to prevent sores from sitting so long in one place. Many individuals with this level of spina bifida are extremely active, as can be seen by the availability of specialty sports chairs for basketball or use on the beach.

Some individuals with spina bifida are unable to use a manual chair and could qualify for a power chair. The requirements and options for power chairs are similar to those discussed in the section on muscular dystrophy. Again, individuals who are wheelchair bound may require special cushioning to prevent sores, and there are special attachments like unique leg rests that help address certain symptoms related to the condition.

There is even adaptive equipment to allow individuals with various forms and levels of spina bifida to do things like swim, bicycle, and ski.

## Common Misconceptions

Many people believe that spina bifida is a death sentence for babies; in fact, some people think the discovery of spina bifida in a fetus is an automatic stillbirth. According to statistics from the CDC, less than five percent of otherwise healthy babies with spina bifida are stillbirths. Additionally, by 1994, medical science was innovative enough to bring 90 percent of babies with spina bifida through their first year of life.

Individuals with spina bifida demonstrate, on average, a normal IQ. In most cases, you would never be able to tell someone had spina bifida, and even those individuals who suffer obvious physical issues are likely to be of average or above average intelligence.

A sac does not always indicate a more severe level of spina bifida. In many cases, symptomology is related to where the defect is located on the spinal column. The higher the defect, the more pervasive any paralysis will be. However, the location of the deformation is not the only contributing factor and should not be used as a sole predictor of how a child with spina bifida will do in life.

# Amputation

Most people probably think of a fully or partially removed arm or leg when they think of amputation. There are actually a number of types — and causes — of amputation.

The first major distinction in amputations is congenital versus acquired amputations. Congenital amputations occur when a baby is born missing all or part of any limb. An acquired amputation involves removing all or part of a limb due to trauma or disease.

### Types of Amputations

- Lower Body
    o Foot or toe amputations, commonly associated with frostbite, traumatic injuries, or diabetes
    o Removal of ankle, known as ankle disarticulation
    o Below-knee amputation, which retains full use of knee
    o Knee-bearing amputation, which is the removal of the entire lower leg at the knee
    o Above knee amputation, which leaves some portion of the thigh present
    o An entire leg amputation, known as a hip disarticulation
- Upper Body
    o Finger or thumb amputation
    o Removal of the hand, or metacarpal amputation
    o Removal of wrist and hand, known as wrist disarticulation
    o Forearm amputation, which leaves some portion of a stump below the elbow

- o Removal at the elbow joint, known as elbow disarticulation
- o Above elbow amputation, which leaves some stump below the shoulder
- o Removal of the entire arm, known as shoulder disarticulation

Amputations can be required in a number of medical situations. Individuals who have experienced severe limb trauma as a soldier, in a natural disaster, or part of a vehicle accident may require amputation because the limb is not salvageable. Diseases and infections can also lead to limb removal. Some medical causes for amputations include:

- Diabetes, which can reduce blood flow to the feet and cause infections or wasting that may require amputation in severe cases
- Buergers disease, which involves painful swelling in the legs
- Gangrene, necrotizing fasciitis, and other infections, which can spread throughout the body if not stopped. If caught early, these infections can often be treated, but untreated, they will rot the infected area until there is no recovery.
- Raynaud's Phenomina, a condition that causes sudden loss of blood flow to extremities.
- Tumors

## Physical Effects

The effects of an amputation depend on how much of the limb was removed. The loss of a single finger isn't going to cause very many problems for an individual, although the loss of several fingers or a thumb may be slightly more problematic. The loss of a foot doesn't impact mobility nearly as much as the loss of an entire leg. Being able to save any amount of the leg below the knee will increase the chance of future mobility with a device, just as the ability to save part of the leg below the hip bone increases stability while sitting and makes it easier to create functional prosthesis for running or walking.

Following a surgical amputation, individuals may experience a fair amount of pain, which is usually managed with medication. This can lead to addictive behavior with regard to the drugs, though that is not common in cases where the patient follows the instructions of healthcare staff.

Medical staff will educate the patient and caregiver about bandaging and caring for a healing amputation; failure to follow through with instructions can result in life-threatening infections. Individuals may be instructed to perform exercises to enhance recovery, and they may also be asked to touch the healing stump to desensitize the area and maintain a sense of touch. For some individuals, this can be extremely difficult; some people may be squeamish, and others may not want to confront the concrete truth of their condition. All the work done following a surgery increases the success rate with a prosthesis or physical therapy later.

In addition to obvious physical effects like loss of motion, balance, or function, individuals who have recently experienced an amputation usually deal with mental effects. Even the loss of something like a finger impacts a person's body image and overall confidence. They may no longer feel like a whole person, may deal with the constant feeling that the limb is still there, and may be overwhelmed with the medical requirements and worry about the future. Over time, many amputees move on from these emotions and are able to live productive, enjoyable lives. Amputees are among some of the most accomplished athletes in the world, having completed in Olympic events, finished triathlons, and climbed some of the world's most famous peaks.

### Equipment and Adaptation

Although there are number of adaptations available for amputees, the most essential item in most cases is a prosthesis. Medical innovations make it possible to replace a growing number of body parts — there are even prosthetic arteries! For amputees, any type of prosthesis will require physical therapy and education; the larger the part being replaced, generally the more education and learning involved in the prosthesis process.

Prostheses have come a long way over the years, but there are still limitations on what a false limb can do. It's hard to make up for the body's natural balance, which means individuals with devices may need to learn basic mobility all over again. Many amputees are unable to bear full body weight on any stump, and it's important to keep the stump and the device clean to avoid infection. Resting frequently and removing the prosthesis periodically also reduces the chance of sores, blister, and cysts.

Prosthetics are available to replace single fingers, hands, arms, legs, and feet. Devices range from basic attachments that help a partial leg or foot amputee to balance to fully functional attachments with working joints. Sports prosthesis often include shock-absorbing designs to allow amputees to run. There are sprinters who can achieve near-record-breaking speeds even though they are missing part of both legs.

In cases where all or a lot of both legs must be removed, the individual may need or prefer a wheelchair. Individuals also missing part or all of either arm may qualify for a power chair, since it would be difficult to self-push a manual wheelchair without full arm functionality.

Amputees can also make individualized adaptations or purchase kits to adapt areas of the home, workspace, or car. Hand control kits allow cars to be operated completely by hand; amputees with one arm stub can use special controls to steer. Specialty equipment for the kitchen or computer allow amputees to cook or work without extra assistance. Depending on the severity and type of amputation, individuals may require walking aids such as crutches, shower chairs and other accessibility devices, and adaptations to basic things like light switches.

### Congenital Amputation

Those who were born with incomplete limbs are more likely to find adaptive equipment an annoyance. From a young age they have learned to move and function with their body as it is, so a prosthesis can feel like it's just getting in the way.

Individuals with incomplete legs may scoot or even sit on a skateboard to get around. Those with incomplete arms or hands are often able to use their stumps to accomplish everyday tasks as effectively as those with unaffected arms and hands.

## Common Misconceptions

Not all amputees want to be part of the Paralympics or be a source of inspiration to everyone around them. This may be obvious, but it also seems like every story about amputees follows this formula. In most cases, amputees who acquired the disability through injury or infection just want to find the best way to return to their normal lives, be accepted by loved ones, and move forward with normal, everyday successes.

Prosthesis are wonderful, and medical innovation has made a lot of progress in the past few decades. However, a prosthesis is not always appropriate or even possible for an amputee. There has to be something to attach the device to; an at-the-knee amputation may seem like the best place to handle lower-leg trauma, but the knee stump can be very difficult to attach a prosthesis to.

There may also be misconceptions surrounding the receipt of a prosthetic limb. Although there are some pre-fab options, it isn't like buying a shoe. The patient has to be precisely measured; in some cases, molds of the stump or amputation site are taken. Experts create a prosthesis from scratch or customize an existing unit to each individual patient. The process can be time-consuming and very expensive, making it hard for everyone in this situation to afford a good or high-end device.

Despite what television ER-dramas might say, it's not always the first choice to salvage a limb, and doing so can endanger the overall health and life of the patient. The decision about amputation must come after full medical evaluation and a comprehensive discussion between the doctor and the patient or patient's family. The patient or family must weigh the emotional, physical, and social consequences of losing a limb with what could be equally or more dire medical consequences associating with keeping a limb. A wasted limb may never recover, hampering the person's movement forever. Even more dangerous, the limb could spread infection to vital organs, which can lead to severe health issues or death. Infection that spreads up a limb or to other limbs can increase the amount of amputation that must be done or lead to the loss of other appendages.

Not all amputees experience a severe sense of loss or require counseling; almost all amputees will agree that they don't want pity. As in any life situation, some individuals are able to adapt more quickly. It's important to consider your character's background when having him adapt to an amputation. Did he work in a line of business—like law enforcement or the armed forces—where traumatic injury was always a possibility, or is he an accountant from the suburbs who was in a car accident? What in his life has prepared him for this challenge, and how will that impact how he reacts to it?

# Spinal Cord Injury

A spinal cord injury interrupts the flow of signals from the brain through the spinal cord and throughout the rest of your body. Because the spinal cord is actually a group of nerves that runs from your brain through your back, it acts a lot like the communication server for your entire body. An injury to that server will result in loss of communication to parts of your body.

There are two overall types of spinal cord injury: incomplete and complete. A complete SCI completely destroys the communication at the injury site, resulting in loss of communication — and thus paralysis — everywhere below that site. An incomplete injury does not fully disrupt communication, which can lead to varying degrees of communication — and thus, movement — below the site.

In many cases, people think of trauma-induced SCI, but damages can also be done to the spinal cord by disease or infection.

The location of the injury determines the level and type of SCI a person is diagnosed with. Injuries from level C1 to T1 are labeled as tetraplegia — commonly called quadriplegia. Individuals with tetraplegia may experience loss of sensation and paralysis of the upper torso and neck, arms, and legs.

Injury lower on the spinal column—from T2 to S5—results in paraplegia, which impacts sensation in and mobility of the legs, hips, stomach, and chest. Each condition has different severity levels, which means a paraplegic with a complete lower injury may only lose functioning in his or her legs.

## Physical Effects

After the first few months of injury, the effects of the SCI become stable and change very little for the rest of the person's life.

You can probably imagine some of the obvious effects of a complete SCI. Individuals usually use wheelchairs for mobility. Paraplegics, who are often able to use all functionality in the upper body, are generally able to live fully functional lives without assistance. With the proper adaptations, a paraplegic can live alone, take care of almost all individual needs, participate in sports and recreational activities, and work in a variety of jobs.

Normal routines are much more challenging for quadriplegics, since they may have lost functionality of all limbs and some areas of the torso. Modern innovation makes it possible for these individuals to engage in daily life, but they are more likely to require assistance with essential activities than someone who has full strength and use of the arms. However, with proper support, a quadriplegic can also participate in recreational activities and work a number of jobs (usually office-based work).

Loss of motion is only the most obvious symptom of an SCI. Both the urinary and bowel systems can suffer from an SCI, depending on where the injury is located. The bladder can become either hyperactive or flaccid due to lack of communication with the brain. A hyperactive — or spastic — bladder leads to incontinence; this can sometimes be treated with medication or surgery. A flaccid bladder doesn't have the right muscle control to void, so it can expand to dangerous levels. Certain devices and procedures may need to be employed to void the bladder periodically to avoid health risks.

The bowel undergoes similar issues following an SCI. In some cases, the injury may create a reflex bowel, which means the bowel will automatically empty itself when full. This can be managed by timing to allow the bowel to empty at a time and place that's socially acceptable. In more severe cases, a flaccid bowel may require extra work or intervention to empty.

Individuals with SCI may also be at risk for high blood pressure, respiratory failure, and digestion problems. Depending on what part of the body is receiving brain communication, it can be difficult for those with SCI to accomplish common tasks like eating. Autonomic dysreflexia is a condition involving an overactive nervous system. Individuals with injuries above the T-5 location are most at risk for autonomic dysreflexia, which causes abrupt spikes in blood pressure. The high blood pressure can cause stroke or seizures if not managed properly, and this condition has led to death for some individuals with SCI. It can be triggered by a number of different things, including the body being uncomfortable and not being able to signal that in another way (since the individual would be unable to feel things such as a lump in his or her seat or the body overheating).

The spine plays an important role in communicating and managing the groups of muscles that control breathing. Spinal cord injuries above a certain level reduce control over the respiratory muscles; complete injuries to the higher areas of the spine could result in a person being placed on a permanent ventilator to force air in and out of the lungs. Portable ventilator systems allow individuals with such conditions to move and they are usually part of a power chair design, but they are quite expensive.

Individuals with spinal cord injuries may experience spasms in their paralyzed limbs. This can be exacerbated by stress or may be a symptom of a larger problem (someone who is paralyzed may not realize if they have injured a limb or sustained a burn). Sometimes in people with incomplete injuries, it may be a signal from the brain that is not getting through properly. People who frequently experience spasms are likely to have less atrophy in those limbs than those who do not. Most people with spinal cord injuries will have some amount of muscle atrophy, making the paralyzed limbs appear thinner than average limbs. Individuals with a higher level of injury may have paralysis of the abdominal muscles, resulting in a bulge in the stomach area.

One area that can be drastically impacted by an SCI is sexual activity. In many cases, men with SCI experience some level of erectile dysfunction, or ED. Some men may not be able to get an erection at all, while others are unable to sustain a full erection long enough to engage in sex. The majority of men with SCI lose the ability to ejaculate, although that doesn't mean they can't experience and enjoy sex.

It does mean that they are often not able to father children through traditional means. There are medical interventions for ED issues, and men with an SCI can also experience sexual satisfaction in nontraditional ways. Some men with SCI take Viagra or a related pill or injection. Others use a vacuum pump to get an erection. Some men are able to get hard through touch (while sexy imagery will not have any effect).

Women with any type of SCI can engage in sex and have children. There are some issues that women should be educated about regarding the difference between an SCI pregnancy and a standard pregnancy, and it's important for women to be treated by an OB/GYN experienced with SCI.

Both men and women may struggle with emotional and mental blocks to sex. Limited mobility means that the individual will need an understanding and open-minded partner. A satisfactory sex life for both individuals is possible, but may require thinking outside of the box and using assistive equipment for positioning. Most people with severe and complete spinal cord injuries are not able to move parts of their body, so partners may have to adjust limbs appropriately, help their partner in or out of bed, and maintain top positions during most sexual activity.

SCI also affects sweat and people are generally not able to sweat below the level of their injury. This can mean the body is unable to regulate its temperature and the individual may overheat easily.

People with incomplete spinal cord injuries may have very different physical challenges. We are used to thinking of a paralyzed person as requiring a wheelchair, but this is not always the case. There is a condition known as "walking quad" in which an incomplete quadriplegic can still walk. The signals from his or her brain to the rest of the body are confused, but not entirely cut off. Such a person may have symptoms like as a dramatic limp, weak hands, and/or a spastic bladder.

## Equipment and Adaptation

The type of equipment required for someone with SCI will depend on the severity of the injury and what function the person has lost. Almost all individuals with a complete SCI will require a wheelchair. Paraplegics usually use a manual wheelchair that allows them to propel themselves from place to place. In fact, since most paraplegics have functional use of arms and shoulders, they don't qualify for insurance-purchased power chairs, and many would not want a power chair as it would be giving up part of their individual functionality.

Power chairs are available for those that have neither the use of their legs or their arms or shoulders. Depending on a person's needs, a power chair can have touch controls with joystick steering or mouth controls that respond to voice or breath. Wheelchairs may have motorized leg and arm lifts, as well as motorized back recliners, all of which are controlled by the most appropriate device for the individual.

Wheelchairs may require special transportation devices. Vehicles can be outfitted with ramps, larger-than-normal doors, or flat floor space to accommodate wheelchairs. In some cases, the car can be retrofitted so that someone in a wheelchair can sit in the front seat and drive using hand controls. Many paraplegics with small manual wheelchairs can use regular cars that have been fitted with hand controls. They are able to transfer into the driver's seat and disassemble the wheelchair to sit in the passenger or back seat.

Someone who sits in a wheelchair all day is likely to develop pressure sores, so it's important to have the right seat and back cushions. There are also gel, foam, and air cushions for beds, which are used for a fully paralyzed individual who spends a lot of time laying still in bed. People with paraplegia are taught to relieve pressure on their butt and thighs by pushing against their chair and lifting their butt for a few seconds frequently throughout the day. People with quadriplegia are told to tilt their power chair back far enough to lift their butt and thighs off the seat of their chair throughout the day.

Lifestyle aids are also available for a variety of purposes. Penis pumps and female stimulators help couples achieve satisfactory intimate relationships; special exercise equipment helps individuals with SCI maintain muscle tone. Ramps and lifts ensure access to home and work; and bars, chairs, and other bathroom accommodations help individuals with SCI maintain personal hygiene. Splints worn on affected hands can help hold utensils, pens, or tools.

## Common Misconceptions

Many people don't realize the level to which individuals with all types of spinal cord injuries continue to live. SCI very rarely affects brain functioning, so individuals still have all the dreams, desires, and thoughts they had before the injury. They still want to have a career, learn new things, or be involved in society. In some cases, it may require a bit of help, and in almost all cases, it will require adaptation and technology, but people with SCI can live happy, adjusted, and full lives.

Most people assume that all paraplegics and quadriplegics must use wheelchairs at all times. With incomplete SCIs, this isn't always the case. In many cases, individuals are able to function with the assistance of canes, crutches, or walkers, and they maintain a range of mobility and motion.

The fact that suicide rates for individuals with SCI are higher than overall averages make people think that all individuals with SCI are depressed. In reality, somewhere between 11 and 37 percent of those with an SCI suffer from clinical depression; when comparing that to the 20 percent overall average in the country, it's apparent that depression rates within the SCI population are likely not exceptionally higher than normal. With proper support, even someone with a very high level of injury can adjust to his or her new normal.

# Misconceptions to Avoid When Writing Disabled Characters into Your Story

Specific misconceptions related to each disability were touched upon in the previous sections, but what about misconceptions regarding disability in general? Fiction writers and story creators seem to love using disabilities in the same metaphors and stereotypical plots. Not only do you want to avoid what others have already done to death, you also want to create organic characters with depth. That means avoiding some common misconceptions and writing crutches associated with disabled characters.

## Disability Shouldn't Be a Surface Metaphor

While there may be some value in using a character's disability as some sort of metaphor, make it unique, meaningful, and realistic to the character and situation. Don't use a disability as a metaphor to show the reader that the character is messed up or struggling with life. First of all, the vast majority of disabled individuals are no more messed up than everyone else. Second, you can convey that a character is struggling without putting him in a wheelchair or giving him a hearing impairment.

As a writer, you have the same obligation to a disabled character that you have to any other character in your story. He or she needs a history, a personality, strengths, weaknesses, desires, and challenges. In short, the character needs to be well rounded. And it's cheating to make his or her only weaknesses the physical issues associated with the disability. Doesn't the character have emotions? Anger, fear, or arrogance? He or she needs strengths and weaknesses that are related to the disability, certainly, but also those that are not. And don't assume that because your character has a disability, he or she must be depressed, angry, or bitter. People respond in a wide variety of ways to disabling circumstances.

## Disabled People Have Just as Much on Their Minds as Anyone Else

Imagine that you're writing a story and you create a character. You decide she's going to be a cheerleader. After that, does every thought, action, and word from this character involve the cheerleading squad? Only if you've purposely set out to create a caricature to make a point or create comedy.

That same premise holds true with disabled characters. If it all revolves around the disability, then you've only written a flat caricature. A disabled person has to live from day to day; he or she wants friendship, success, and entertainment.
If your story is a mystery, then the disabled character may have a reason to hide the crime or seek the truth about the crime. If it's an action adventure, maybe she's a crack shot with a rifle.

Keep adding to the character until you get a real person. Because disabled people don't constantly think about themselves and their condition, just like a healthy character wouldn't go around describing how great his legs were and how he could walk.

## Disability Isn't a Great Conflict

Yes, the situation surrounding and created by a disability delivers a challenge for your character. Sue, who has MS, is going to have a hard time traveling across the jungle in a day to get a life-saving message to Jimmy. However, the story is in how Sue gets through the jungle despite all of her weaknesses and obstacles — only one of which is MS. The story is not how Sue conquers MS. Because, in most cases, disabilities are part of a person, they aren't an obstacle to be surmounted.

## Get the Sex Right

Admittedly, sex in any fictional situation rarely mimics reality. If you're going to put a disabled character in a sexual situation, though, it pays to at least know the rules before you break them. First, almost all disabled people can engage in sex, even if it takes a little bit of creative problem solving to do so. Just because someone's legs don't work or they're in a wheelchair doesn't mean they can't have sex or that they don't want to have sex. If sex is a natural part of the story, then there's no reason to leave it out.

On the other hand, if there's not a reason to include sex in your story, then don't. There's no need to drive home a point about a character's spinal cord injury by introducing a passage about sexual troubles. There's definitely no need to make a statement by creating a character with a spinal cord injury that has a perfectly functioning penis despite the fact that his legs, bowel, and bladder no longer work fully.

If you decide to include a sex scene, make sure you understand the disability in question and how it will impact physical performance and intimacy.

## Diversity and Community

Disabilities affect people of all ages, races, and genders. Some disabilities impact certain groups more than others, but disability is, overall, diverse. There seems to be a preponderance of rich men with disabilities in fiction. If you're thinking of writing a wheelchair-bound prince or a blind philanthropist into your story, consider carefully. Are you going to make the character unique, or will it be another check mark in the white, male, bitter, arrogant, and wealthy column?

Another thing to avoid is the metaphor of alienation many like to tack onto disabled individuals. Characters that grow up in a small community where no one understands them or where individuals walk on the other side of the road for fear of "catching" the disability are certainly out-of-date, if not completely clichéd.

In reality, disabled characters know other people with disabilities. At the same time, they aren't going to be friends with every other person with a disability in a ten mile radius. If they've got nothing else in common, why would they be friends? (Maybe they're all part of the same sport's team? Keep thinking outside the box!)

## People with Disabilities Are Biased Too

People who acquire disabilities later in life have spent years thinking about disability exactly the way you do now. Sometimes it takes a while for the switch to flip in someone's mind to realize that they are now disabled themselves.

Sometimes people get comfortable with their own disabilities but are prejudiced against others. There can sometimes be a sense of hierarchy among people who have disabilities. Someone who is a paraplegic, for example, may have incorrect and cliché ideas about the life of a quadriplegic. Someone with vision loss might have no idea how someone who uses a wheelchair functions day to day.

Knowing one disability doesn't mean understanding all of them or being welcoming and inclusive to all.

# Not Everyone Has A Perfect Set Up

The equipment and adaptations meant to increase quality of life for disabled individuals are expensive. It's rare for someone to have insurance that covers all devices, and in many cases, individuals may be on Medicare and/or Medicaid, which could limit access to equipment even more. If there is the ability to pay for equipment, most families or individuals will make that choice, because the equipment and adaptations make life so much easier for everyone involved. When doors are wide enough for wheelchairs, for example, a disabled person can move freely about the house.

As you write, be cognizant of the cost of the equipment you're including in your story. A poor farm family isn't going to have the latest equipment. There are grant programs for adaptations, and community organizations may donate toward a cause, so there may be an explanation for why your young, orphaned college student could afford a power chair and ramp to his apartment. Just make sure you, as the author, know how all that equipment got there. You don't even have to address it in the story. By understanding it yourself, the presence of the equipment in your story will be that much more believable.

## The Disability Isn't the Story

Granted, in some cases you may be writing the story of the disability and recovery. But in most cases, you're writing a different story that happens to have a disabled character in it. This is like having a character with any other trait—a mother who lost a child, an alcoholic, a man who just sold his first book, a child who has discovered the world outside his backyard. All of those things impact how the character deals with and reacts to things in the story, but none of those is *the story*. As important, none of those *is the character*.

A mother who lost a child is still a woman. Perhaps she's an accountant. She's also a wife, a daughter, a sister, and a volunteer at the local animal shelter. All of these are going to come through in the story, as well as her grief.

A disabled person may be an amputee with a prosthetic leg. But he's also a dentist, an uncle, a boyfriend, and an occasional thief. But only penny candy from the corner store, because he doesn't really need money and he's only doing it for the rush. He doesn't want to steal anything of value, because the storeowner's a decent guy.

Within a few sentences, I've created the start of a story that's not about a disability but features a character that's so much *more* than his disability.

## Disabled Villains Should Be Believable Villains

There's nothing that says your disabled character has to be the hero. Maybe she's the villain of your story; if that's the case, make sure she's a believable bad guy. Just because she's in a wheelchair or missing an arm doesn't make her bad. Taking the easy way out and blaming her anger and villainy on the disability or the cause of the disability is almost cheating.

Instead, dig deeper. Maybe the disability plays some role in her move to the dark side, but she had to be leaning that way anyway. What in her history or personality makes her a candidate for villainy? The best villains all went wrong for a reason. Darth Vader let his fear overtake his love, and he was swayed to the dark side to save his lover. He was disabled, but how often does the story dwell on that? Other villains go bad for money, fame, or power. Others are mentally deranged and just like the feeling they get when they make others suffer. Whatever it is about your character, give them a good reason to go bad.

## Check Your Privilege

Really stop to examine your assumptions about disability. Did you know that not all people who are paralyzed have a goal of walking? Not everyone defines recovery in the same way and plenty of people don't think walking is a measure of success in life. Others do.

Everyone is going to think about and respond to disability differently so be sure to take the time to get to know your character well enough to know how he or she will respond to a disability.

Human beings are remarkably adaptable. Even if you can't imagine dealing with vision loss or being on a ventilator, don't assume you wouldn't adapt to it just fine. Most people in those situations do. Particularly if given proper support and resources, there's nothing people can't build a life with.

It really does become normal and just part of life. You go back to worrying about what you've always worried about: performance reviews at work, whether your spouse is doing his or her share, conferences with the kids' teachers, etc.

## Look Deeper

Always look deeper to avoid the fictional misconceptions associated with disabled characters. When you look deeper, you look beyond the disability. Just like in real life, when you look past the surface and get to know someone for who they are inside, you might be surprised at what your character has to tell you. Chances are, very little of it will directly involve his or her physical issues.

It's a balance you need to strike. You don't want to gloss over physical challenges the character faces but you also don't want the story to turn into nothing but a long list of things she can't do (or thinks she can't do). Most people don't realize just how much a person with a disability can do but at the same time it's good to show a little of *how* they do those things rather than having a character who uses a wheelchair able to go and visit all his friends and never mention how he deals with the stairs.

For any action you want your character with a disability to take, he or she almost certainly can do it. You just have to figure out how and with what adaptations within his or her constraints.

# Playing with Stereotypes, or, The Last Thing Anyone Expects

One way to have a lot of fun and ensure you don't fall into fictional clichés about disabilities is to turn stereotypes around. Whether the person in question is a main character, a sidekick, or a marginal character, you can create a unique, memorable person by doing the last thing anyone expects.

Perhaps you're writing the story of Rose, a young woman who has lost her parents and, on a whim, purchased a rambling property she loved as a child. The property's in disrepair, and perhaps there's a ghost, or hidden treasure, or an attic filled with thousands of hats, all of which tell a different story. That thing — the ghost, treasure, hat library — is what's going to fuel your plot.

But Rose needs another character to play off of. It's easy to bring in a handyman — or handywoman — to play the part. There's an organic need for that character in the story, since you've already created a setting that needs work. This handyman or woman is a jack-of-all-trades, a passable carpenter, and quick with a paint roller. Oh, and he, or she, uses a wheelchair.

Having the wheelchair-using character perform a fairly physical job turns the stereotype on its head. Notice, however, that the stereotype flip isn't some gimmick that's supposed to drive the story. In most cases, gimmicks don't work. In fact, the flip isn't even *that* relevant to the story. It will, however, add a lot of depth and authenticity.

There's a lot you, as a writer, can do with this situation that will interest the reader. But at no point does the handyperson's disability become the major obstacle or plot point.

What if you want the disability to play a bigger role in the plot? You can apply the same idea. Consider Jack, a blind man who grew up on the Gulf Coast. Jack's family has been in the fishing industry for over a hundred years; his dad is the last fisherman and captains the last family boat. And he wants to pass on the family business to Jack.

Okay, here, you can do several things. Perhaps Jack has been fishing for years, despite being blind, and he wants to take on the company business. That's a pretty big stereotype flip for a blind character. Now, you have to throw some conflict Jack's way. Is it a man versus nature story? Does he get caught in a storm or deal with a boat wreck? Perhaps it's a man versus man story, where Jack must prove himself as captain to the crew.

Notice how it's never a man versus disability story?

Suppose Jack *doesn't* want to take over the family business. Stereotyping would mean you make that decision about the fact that Jack is blind and doesn't think he's capable of doing the job. There are other reasons Jack might not want to take over the business. Maybe Jack dreams of being an artist, or he's graduated at the top of his class and is on the way to law school.

Whatever the reason, turn the stereotype on its head.

# Prompts for Playing with Stereotypes

Take a few moments to play with some stereotypes to get your creativity flowing. Use what you've learned about some disabilities in this book to fill in the prompts below with some situations that don't follow stereotypes.

1. Lisa is deaf and is a student. Describe what she looks like, who her best friend is, and the activity she's going to be involved with after school today. (Hint: Don't make it sign language club.)

2. Malcolm lost part of his leg; he's in his thirties and lives in downtown Miami. There's been a murder in his apartment. Describe Malcolm's role in the activities of the day and how he interacts with the rest of the tenants. (Hint: Don't make Malcolm the victim of the situation.)

3. Landra has cerebral palsy and works in a high-rise building. Describe what Landra does for a living and write a few paragraphs about what happened when she got to work this morning. (Hint: Don't make Landra a social worker or a lab tech working for a company that's going to come up with a cure.)

4. Alvin has a spinal cord injury and he's being released from the county jail. Someone's outside waiting for him. Why was Alvin in jail, and who's waiting for him outside? Are they happy to see him, and how will he feel when he sees them? (Hint: Don't put Alvin in jail because he caused an accident, which also put him in a wheelchair.)

## Integration is Always Important

It's fun to play with stereotypes, but always remember to integrate elements of your character into the story. Don't select an occupation, characteristic, or situation simply because it flies in the face of stereotype. Every decision must advance the plot, reveal the character, or create suspense. Simply throwing in that your deaf character is a pro on the piano doesn't do anything unless it is revealing something particular about her character or there's a reason someone in the story has to play piano. Think "Goonies," but with a deaf girl saving the day in the organ scene.

# Clichés in Fiction

When it comes to disabilities in books, stories, movies, and television, clichés abound. This section will lay out some of the most used clichés so you can avoid writing them into your story.

**The Hidden Truth**
The storyline that involves a blind person who hides his disability from everyone (or one particular character) has been done. A lot. It's also not very realistic. It's actually very difficult for a blind person to fake being sighted. Blind eyes may roll or shift, will show scarring, and will never focus on anything.

This cliché goes the other way too; the sighted character is disfigured or ugly and hides this truth from the blind character, who is the only one who could love someone so hideous. Perhaps the love interest or other character isn't disfigured, but there's a reason for the identity to remain hidden. A girl breaks up with her boyfriend over his commitment issues, and then she's blinded in an accident. He moves into the apartment next door and strikes up a friendship with her; she falls in love with him, never realizing who he is. Because, you know...she didn't date him for years and wouldn't recognize his voice or mannerisms. It doesn't take a blind person to be able to recognize a person by voice — people all over the world do it every day when speaking on the phone.

This idea is so overdone that it's been the premise for several Disney Channel show episodes, including an episode of *ANT Farm*. If your overall premise is showing up on cookie-cutter preteen television, it might be time to come up with a new angle.

## The Resentful Cripple
The disease, disability, or situation has made the character bitter and resentful. He or she is mean-spirited and cynical. It might make for a few great one-liners, but it also makes for a character that has one side. Yes, your character may be resentful because of his situation, but there's more to him than that. Make him three-dimensional by exploring other feelings and activities.

## The Resentful Love Interest
Possibly worse than the resentful disabled character is the resentful disabled guy who hates the world until the perfect woman comes along. He heaps abuse on her, draws away, is wishy-washy because of past rejection, but she's an angel of perfection whose only mission is to draw her crabby love interest out of his shell. First, no one is that perfect. Second, not only is this a fictional disability cliché, it's also a cliché in general fiction and media. From *Fifty Shades of Grey* to *As Good as It Gets*, this one's been done.

## The Blind Driver
This one's been in at least a dozen movies. You have to ask yourself: What, really, would motivate a blind man or woman to get into the driver's seat? And, outside of placing the scene in a giant cornfield in Iowa, how does it ever end well?

## The Blind Expressionist
Blind eyes are typically scarred or out of focus. The hero isn't going to look into the angry eyes of his blind lover and see the storm of her emotions.

## The Sketchy Accident or Illness

Imagine you're writing a science fiction story. There's going to be an alien...of some kind. It's important to the story, so you just write him in. You don't really know how he got there, but you assume it was a spaceship of some sort.

Realistically, that's not how a good science fiction writer does things. The reader may not know, but the author knows how the alien came to earth and why. Just like you should know how the character came by his or her disability. Don't create vague details about why the person is in a wheelchair or is blind. In a contemporary story, if the person was born with the disability, medical science can explain it and so should you. Do the research to find out how an accident can cause complete blindness or put someone in a wheelchair. In a historical setting, use something appropriate for that time period — which may be very different from what would happen today.

For example, a character in a car accident is much more likely to sustain injuries related to a SCI or amputation than to be struck completely blind.

This doesn't mean you need to include it in the story. If it's not relevant to the plot, it doesn't have to come up. But you as the author should still know. It will affect other choices you make for that character.

## The Lip-Reader That Saves the Day

From across the crowded office — through a glass window, no less — Susan, the deaf secretary, lip-reads to find out all about the plot to subvert her boss and endanger the public with low-quality goods.

Maybe you really want Susan to save the day, but lip reading may not be the right choice. According to experts, lip reading is an extremely rare skill, and even those who are able to do it well don't achieve extremely high levels of accuracy.

It's more likely that Susan will discover the treachery the way any other secretary would: through seeing a communication she wasn't meant to see via email, fax, or a paper lying on someone's desk. It's even more likely that the villains disregard Susan as a threat due to her disability and talk openly around her so much that she's able to put together some suspicions based on body language and situational context.

## Misunderstandings about Deaf Speakers
Individuals who have been deaf since birth are not going to have perfect speech patterns. They've never heard what speech is supposed to sound like. People who developed deafness recently may have perfectly formed speech, but have trouble finding the right volume or tone since they can't hear themselves.

## The Sexual Prowess of the SCI Guy
Someone with a spinal cord injury is not going to be Lady Chatterley's Lover. Yes, someone with SCI can be sexually active. They can even be sexually attractive. But, statistics seem to indicate that there might be a few bumps on the road to the bedroom, and those are bumps you as the author need to deal with.

If you're going to go there with your characters, then you need to do the research to understand what a spinal cord injury — or any other disability — means for physical intimacy.

In real life, couples seek out alternative methods of satisfaction or work together to find the right movements or positions. Realistic sex doesn't have to be weird; highlighting the developing relationship rather than the physical equipment is actually a great way to heat up the scene.

### The Blind Leading the Blind

In reality, a person leads a blind individual by allowing the blind person to hold onto an elbow. The sighted person steps forward, and the blind person is slightly to the side and behind them. You would rarely lead a blind person by holding hands and pulling or taking hold of his or her elbow and pushing. Having your blind hero lead the sighted heroine into the ballroom while her arm is resting through his elbow is a bit unrealistic. It might work, if he was leading her through his own home and there were no other people around.

### The Out-of-Time Know How

Historical fiction is extremely dependent on good research, and the same holds true for disabled characters in historical settings. Everything in this book applies to today. Most of the devices and procedures discussed are modern inventions. Even the canes described for blind individuals were only developed in the latter half of the 20th century. Prior to that, the canes were very different.

Having a character with some of these disabilities in historical settings is actually fairly impossible. Someone born in the 17th century with a severe form of spina bifida would be unlikely to survive birth or even infancy.

A complete injury to the spine in a medieval setting would likely be a death sentence without modern medical care.

Not only would there be no modern medication or surgical process, but there'd be no way to handle bladder or other issues. If the individual survived the trauma, he or she would probably die as the body slowly poisoned itself.

**The Injury-Recovery Story**
Yes, there's a place and time for the injury-recovery story or the coping-with-a-new-disability story, but the majority of people living with disabilities are not living that story. In the overall lifespan of disabled individuals, the recovery or coping period can be fairly small. Always choosing to write about this time period is like always choosing to write about high school graduation. There are some good stories to tell, but a lot of them have been told.

In telling your story, consider branching into other areas. What about the person who's been disabled for life or who has been disabled for ten years and has learned to cope?

In writing the injury-recovery story, you're making the disability the story. That's not always a bad thing, but make sure that's really where you want to take your story before you go there.

# Conclusion

Now that you understand some good reasons for including disabled characters in your story, you may be teeming with new fiction ideas. Follow the guidelines in this book to portray disabilities with accuracy and sensitivity. Not only will you tell a better story, you'll also help people with disabilities to get the fair treatment and portrayal they deserve.

Obviously this book only covers a handful of well-known physical disabilities. There are many more types of physical disabilities as well as emotional disabilities, learning disabilities, invisible disabilities, mental disabilities, etc. Hopefully we can create resource guides for many of those as well! Still, many of the tips in the second half of this book should help you with those types of disabilities also.

Our mission statement at Dev Love Press is that the more books there are with realistic portrayals of disability, the more people will understand how to interact with disabled individuals in their everyday life. More realistic disability in fiction means less fear and misunderstanding in the world and that can only be a good thing!

Once you can write about disabilities in an accurate, interesting, and compelling fashion, you're ready to complete your manuscript. When you do, be sure to submit it to Dev Love Press!

# Resources

A great way to get detailed information and opinions about particular disabilities is to read autobiographies of people who have the disabilities you are writing about.

Here are some recommendations:

**Still Me** by Christopher Reeve: Quadriplegia
**Moving Violations** by John Hockenberry: Paraplegia
**The Man Who Walked In His Head** by Patrick Segal: Paraplegia
**Double Take: A memoir** by Kevin Michael Connolly: Congenital Amputee
**And There Was Light** by Jacques Lusseyran: Blindness
**I'll Do It Myself** by Glenda Watson Hyatt: Cerebral Palsy
**Soul Surfer** by Bethany Hamilton: Amputation
**The Story of My Life** by Helen Keller: Deafblindness (Don't watch the movie; get the story from its source!)
**What's That Pig Outdoors?** By Henry Kisor: Deafness
**Deaf in America: Voices from a culture** by Carol Padden and Tom Humphries: Deafness

www.ingramcontent.com/pod-product-compliance
Lightning Source LLC
Chambersburg PA
CBHW050549280326
41933CB00011B/1779